AF270633

BUFFALO BILLS

KENNY ABDO

abdobooks.com

Published by Abdo Zoom, a division of ABDO, P.O. Box 398166, Minneapolis, Minnesota 55439. Copyright © 2022 by Abdo Consulting Group, Inc. International copyrights reserved in all countries. No part of this book may be reproduced in any form without written permission from the publisher. Fly!™ is a trademark and logo of Abdo Zoom.

Printed in the United States of America, North Mankato, Minnesota.
052021
092021

Photo Credits: AP Images, Getty Images, iStock, Newscom, Shutterstock PREMIER
Production Contributors: Kenny Abdo, Jennie Forsberg, Grace Hansen
Design Contributors: Candice Keimig, Neil Klinepier

Library of Congress Control Number: 2020919468

Publisher's Cataloging-in-Publication Data

Names: Abdo, Kenny, author.
Title: Buffalo Bills / by Kenny Abdo
Description: Minneapolis, Minnesota : Abdo Zoom, 2022 | Series: NFL teams |
    Includes online resources and index.
Identifiers: ISBN 9781098224547 (lib. bdg.) | ISBN 9781098225483 (ebook) |
    ISBN 9781098225957 (Read-to-Me ebook)
Subjects: LCSH: Buffalo Bills (Football team)--Juvenile literature. | National Football
    League--Juvenile literature. | Football teams--Juvenile literature. | American
    football--Juvenile literature. | Professional sports--Juvenile literature.
Classification: DDC 796.33264--dc23

TABLE OF CONTENTS

BUFFALO BILLS

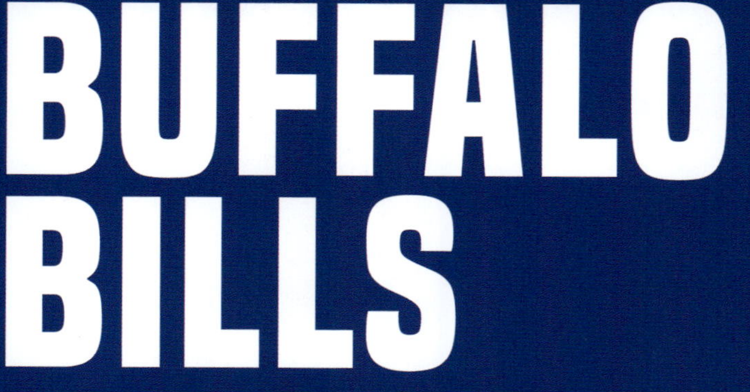

Sporting the signature red, white, and blue, the Buffalo Bills are one of America's longest-running football teams.

New York state can get frigidly cold.
But Buffalo Bill fans will brave any
weather to support their team.

KICK OFF

Businessman Ralph C. Wilson Jr. founded the Buffalo Bills in 1959. Wilson was part of the Foolish Club, a group of AFL owners. The club got its name for being idiotic enough to take on the NFL.

The team played its first game the
next year. In 1962, fullback Cookie
Gilchrist was the first AFL player to
run for more than 1,000 yards in a
season.

The Bills tied with the Boston Patriots for the best record in the AFL Eastern Division in 1963. They won their division the next two years. The Bills beat the San Diego Chargers both times in the AFL **championship**!

TEAM RECAPS

In 1970, the AFL joined the NFL. The Bills struggled to win. For the next 18 years, they only made it to the playoffs three times.

From 1988 to 1995, the Bills won five **AFC** Eastern Division titles. They became the only team to play in four straight **Super Bowls**! However, there would be no wins.

The Giants beat the Bills at **Super Bowl** XXV by just one point! They then lost Super Bowl XXVI to Washington. While Super Bowls XXVII and XXVIII went to the Cowboys.

The Bills finished the 2019 season with a 10–6 record. They lost the **wild card** playoffs to the Texans. Cornerback Tre'Davious White was named one of the **AP All-Pros**.

In 2020, Josh Allen quickly moved from backup to starting **quarterback** and team captain. For the first time in the team's history, the Bills swept their division.

HALL OF FAME

Jim Kelly led the Bills to the playoffs eight times and four consecutive **Super Bowls** in his 11 seasons. He also led the NFL in passing in 1990 and the **AFC** in 1991. Kelly was **inducted** into the Pro Football Hall of Fame in 2002.

Thurman Thomas rushed for more than 1,000 yards in eight consecutive seasons with the Bills. Only four other players have done that in NFL history! Thomas was named NFL **MVP** in 1991. He was **inducted** into the Pro Football Hall of Fame in 2007.

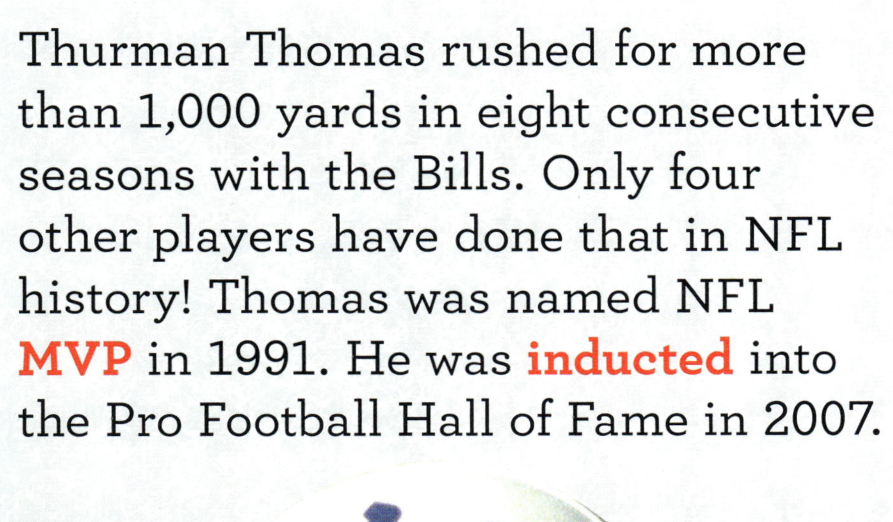

In his 15 seasons with the Bills, Bruce Smith became NFL's all-time **sack** leader with 200. He was named **AFC** Defensive Player of the Year four times and NFL Defensive Player of the Year twice. Smith was **inducted** into the Pro Football Hall of Fame in 2009.

GLOSSARY

American Football Conference (AFC) – one of two major conferences of the NFL. Each conference contains 16 teams split into four divisions. The winner of the AFC championship plays the NFC.

AP All-Pro – an honor given by press organizations to professional NFL players that names the best player at each position during a season.

championship – a game held to find a first-place winner.

induct – to admit someone as a member of an organization.

MVP – short for "most valuable player," an award given in sports to a player who has performed the best in a game or series.

quarterback – the player on the offensive team that directs teammates in their play.

sack – when a quarterback is tackled behind the line of scrimmage while still in possession of the ball.

Super Bowl – the NFL championship game, played once a year.

Wild Card Round – the first round of the playoffs. Each of the two conferences send four division champions and three wild-card teams to its postseason.

ONLINE RESOURCES

Booklinks
NONFICTION NETWORK
FREE! ONLINE NONFICTION RESOURCES

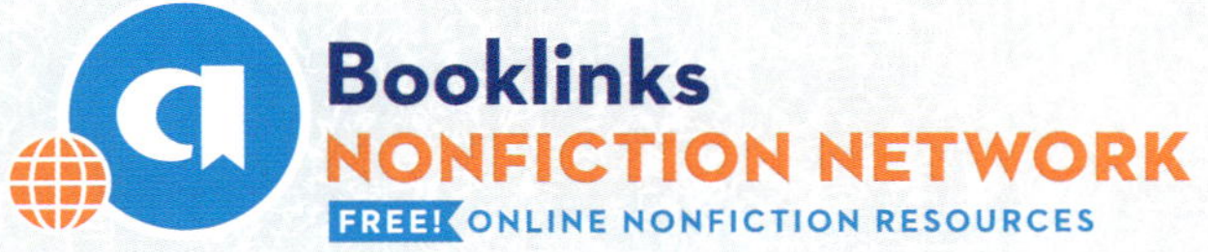

To learn more about the Buffalo Bills, please visit **abdobooklinks.com** or scan this QR code. These links are routinely monitored and updated to provide the most current information available.

INDEX